In His Ele

THE ART AND SCIENCE OF R

Alan Marshall **Mascot Media**

Published in Great Britain in 2012 by Mascot Media Ltd, Norfolk, UK.
Website: www.mascotmedia.co.uk Email: mascot_media@btinternet.com

A CIP catalogue record for this book is available from the British Library.
ISBN: 978-0-9571811-1-3

Photographs from Roger Cockram, the author's personal archive, or other sources as
identified.

Designed by Mascot Media. Edited by Marion Scott.

Printed by Henry Ling Ltd, 23 High East Street, Dorchester, Dorset DT1 1HD.
Email: enquiries@henryling.co.uk

DEDICATIONS

Thanks to Roger for his full support and co-operation. Great pots and a great potter.
Also to Ros, for her warm hospitality and good company.
Our gratitude to Nick Garner, who introduced us to Roger's work and still champions his cause.

PICTURE CAPTIONS

Front cover: *against a backdrop of the North Devon coast at Croyde, a selection of Roger Cockram pots from 2008 to 2012 featuring lobster, seahorse, fish and, most of all, the sea itself*

Title page: *shell form, c.2000*

Page 4: *sea surf bottle, 2011*

Pages 6 & 7: *Roger Cockram at work at the wheel in his Chittlehampton studio*

Pages 8 & 9: *the view from the pottery, April 2012*

Back cover: *Roger working on a large sea surf bottle; the completed pot featuring a spiral of swimming fish through the surf.*

The Art and Science of Roger Cockram

art

noun:

> the expression or application of human creative skill and imagination, typically in a visual form such as painting or sculpture, producing works to be appreciated primarily for their beauty or emotional power.

science

noun:

> the intellectual and practical activity encompassing the systematic study of the structure and behaviour of the physical and natural world through observation and experiment.

Art and science are often portrayed as opposites. However, a combination of the two can be the best of both worlds. Ceramics is the ideal medium for the 'artistic scientist', and Roger Cockram is a prime example of the species.

The scientist in Roger is often sidelined by the artist. Armed with banjo, guitar and a fine singing voice, he seldom misses the opportunity to perform when he isn't throwing pots, peering in rock pools, or tending his allotment.

But whenever there is a more practical challenge at the studio or in his North Devon home, the scientist steps out from the shadows. Faced with a constant quest to hone his pottery skills, the scientist is seldom far away when the kiln requires attention, or new glazes need to be formulated.

Roger's pottery brings together his understanding of nature with his abilities at the wheel. None of the best principles of the craft potter are compromised in his marine-influenced designs. Science and art work in close harmony.

Whether learning a new banjo technique such as 'frailing', or creating a series of pots that portrays the immense power of the sea in a more impressionistic manner, Roger is always on the move. This reflects either the creative urges of his inner artist, or the desire to experiment and explore that is at the heart of every scientist. Whatever the explanation, it has resulted in some spectacular pots.

These pages chart Roger's fascinating journey from Devon schoolboy and science graduate, through Harrow School of Art and his early domestic stoneware, to the increasingly complex individual pieces inspired by a love of the sea and the life it supports.

*I must go down to the seas again, for the call of the running tide
Is a wild call and a clear call that may not be denied;
And all I ask is a windy day with the white clouds flying,
And the flung spray and the blown spume,
and the sea-gulls crying.*

John Masefield

Contents

Looking back at 40 years of throwing, decorating, glazing and firing, Roger sees it as a journey of discovery. At Harrow, he was pushed to make Leach-style pots inspired by the East. He changed to more traditional English techniques with slip trailing, becoming the 'craftsman potter'.

Domestic stoneware gave way to the nature-influenced studio pottery of the 1990s, leading to the Arts and Crafts label that has refused to stick. More modelling, more piercing and more figurative work was the vehicle of the last decade, with the Bonhams exposure providing a valuable push.

The latest evolution isn't a
change of direction, just another bend
in the road, as Roger plots his route through
the rest of the decade. There are still plans for a new kiln,
plenty of shows to attend, lectures to give, demonstrations to
arrange, gigs to play and lots more pots to make.

Barnstaple boy

Much of Roger Cockram's life has been spent within a few miles of his birthplace in Barnstaple, North Devon. The town, a ferocious rival to Bideford across the bay, has a long tradition of pottery production. Barnstaple pottery has been found in archaeological excavations as far away as Maryland in the USA, with the Devon town in the late 16th and early 17th centuries having been a major exporter of ceramic items.

While the major centres for British slipware production in the 17th century were London, Kent and Staffordshire, North Devon had begun to play a significant role through

From boy to man, Roger Cockram has remained loyal to his North Devon roots, absent only for a few years during further education and his early working life

the potteries in Barnstaple and Bideford. The Port Books (locally created records of customs duties paid on overseas trade between 1565 and 1799) list frequent parcels of earthenware being shipped to the USA.

Slipwares are generally earthenware objects decorated with watered-down clays (slip) that have been blended into a creamy liquid for application to the surface of an unfired pot. Glaze is applied and the pot is then fired. Slipwares had largely faded from fashion by the middle of the 18th century, but North Devon continued to produce work of a high standard for at least another 100 years.

In fact, Barnstaple and Bideford potteries refined the pitcher, or harvest jug, concept to such an extent that these full-bellied vessels (with increasingly sophisticated decoration) were to become a recognised art form. They were accompanied by elaborate platters and chargers featuring not only slip-trailed motifs, but complex sgraffito effects where the surface is scraped away to reveal the base colour beneath.

Edwin Beer Fishley at Combrew (just two miles from Barnstaple) followed three previous generations of potters in the small village, and is recognised as one of the most influential mid-19th-century 'peasant potters'. He was trained well in the arts of throwing and slip decoration, and Fishley's earthenware pots were made of clay from the local pits that had supplied the earlier potteries at Barnstaple and Bideford.

There was a ready market for his work among local farmers and well-to-do households in North Devon. Among these were the Cardews, who had a country house at nearby Braunton. As a child, Michael Cardew was taken to see Fishley throwing and to select new pottery from the latest firing. It is known that Fishley inspired

A Barnstaple postcard, dating from around 1958, when the 11-year-old Roger Cockram was growing up in and around the North Devon town. Barnstaple, a ferocious rival to Bideford across the bay, has a long tradition of potters and pottery.

North Devon has for centuries been an important provider of so-called 'ball' clay, which played an important role in the local pottery and brick trade as well as making it a huge supplier to industry. The rich deposits of clay were known for many decades, but were exploited on a meaningful commercial scale only after the arrival of the railways in the 1880s.

Cardew to become a potter, and was later to have a profound impact on the other 'great master', Bernard Leach.

Fishley, who died in 1912, was responsible for distinctive pitchers and platters often featuring lines of folk poetry or hunting scenes, all made using the local Devon clay.

Brannam's is, perhaps, the most famous of late-19th-century North Devon potteries, established in 1847 as a producer of clay sewage pipes and tiles, before Charles Hubert Brannam in 1879 began to experiment with the creation of art pottery at the company's Litchdon Street works. Inspired by nature, much like Roger Cockram a century later, Brannam is known particularly for the use of fish and other sea creatures in his highly decorative art pottery designs.

Charles Brannam can be classified as one of the early 'Arts and Crafts' potters, riding a wave stirred up by William Morris. Brannam was inspired particularly by Barnstaple-born artist Owen Davis, who went on to be an

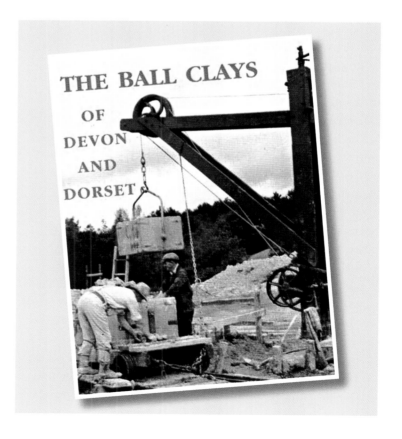

Roger's specialisation in Marine Ecology provided endless opportunities to examine the sea and its contents at close quarters. He became a keen and competent diver, shown here in 1969 with a captured crawfish.

Other exploits included the discovery and salvage of a WWII landing craft, which was subsequently used to take a group of students to the August 1970 Isle of Wight rock festival!

important interior designer in London. Liberty, London's exclusive Regent Street department store, was later to become sole agent for Brannam's pots, eventually assuming control of his designs.

North Devon has for centuries been an important provider of so-called 'ball' clay, which has formed the basis for its local pottery and brick trade as well as making it a huge supplier to industry. The rich deposits of clay were known for many decades, but were exploited on a meaningful commercial scale only after the arrival of the railways in the 1880s.

The ball clays of Devon have been in general use in UK pottery compositions since the latter half of the 17th century. From the middle of the 19th century, they were exported to countries throughout Europe and to the USA. They continue to be marketed throughout the world thanks to their unique and consistent combination of physical properties.

In the north of the country, the clay is won from a deposit located near Peters Marland, about a mile to the east of the village of Petrockstowe (north of Okehampton). To this day, Roger uses only clay from this source at Meeth Quarry, which has been functioning since 1960.

However, the young Roger John Cockram neither emerged from a long line of potters nor had any obvious links with the Petrockstowe Basin. Maybe, at a deep-rooted, subconscious level, he had a predilection for the local clay

and the Devon pottery tradition. If so, it wasn't to manifest itself for another two decades.

His father was a Barnstaple man and his mother a Swansea import, raising Roger as a Methodist with all of the religion's particular trappings. While Roger escaped indoctrination (and declined to be confirmed), he was expected to participate in certain Chapel activities. Joining the choir was no great hardship. His home was full of song, both folk and hymnal. Roger's singing voice survived the rigours of puberty and continues to delight him and his audiences.

Escaping the family pews downstairs, he first joined Great Uncle Tom upstairs with his endless supply of milk chocolate Rolos, before investigating the Chapel's jumble sale contributions in the attic. Here, he was to find his first banjo, which added a new dimension to his musical education.

Science studies

There was no clear plan during schooldays for life after education. Roger hoped perhaps that his time at a rather academic grammar school in Barnstaple would provide some 'easy' choices for sixth form studies.

His initial selection of subjects – Art, English Literature and French – suggests rather Bohemian leanings. The school was having none of it, steering him firmly in the direction of Zoology, Botany and Chemistry. Roger accepted the decision

Roger chose to carry out postgraduate research and a PGCE at Southampton University, working as part of a small team looking at the effect of the new oil-fired Fawley power station on Southampton Water and its occupants

with little argument and prospered in his science studies.

A degree in Zoology at the University of London's Portsmouth Marine Laboratory followed. The facility was at that time situated across the harbour channel on Hayling Island. It had been set up in the 1940s by a brewery chemist from London, Dr J H Oliver, who saw marine biology as an intriguing hobby. In 1967, when Dr Oliver passed away, his wife gave the marine laboratory to the University.

Roger's specialisation in Marine Ecology provided endless opportunities to examine the sea and its contents at close quarters. He became a keen and competent diver, taking every opportunity to explore the seabed and the life it supported. An enduring link with nature was forged. This was to play a major role in the later, more creative career.

After leaving university, he briefly turned his back on science, and spent 12 carefree months as part of a three-piece folk band, gigging regularly and living out of the boot of a car. A career in music was considered, but ultimately rejected. However, Roger continues to enjoy performing locally, singing, playing the banjo and guitar.

Having opted out of a minstrel's varied but uncertain life on the road, he chose instead to acquire a postgraduate

certificate in education at Southampton University, as well as to carry out postgraduate research, working as part of a small team looking at the effect of the new oil-fired Fawley power station on Southampton Water and its inhabitants.

The work was well ahead of its time, in that the team was studying the distribution of a particular type of worm that was extremely sensitive to changes in the environment, making it a very good 'indicator' species. Nowadays this would be seen as vitally important research, backed by plenty of 'green' funding. At the start of the 1970s, however, environmental research was a much lower priority.

While in his early twenties, Roger was inspired by *As I Walked Out One Midsummer Morning* by British poet and author Laurie Lee. In the autobiographical volume, Lee scrapes together a living by playing his violin outside the street cafés of Spain, and sleeps at night in his blanket under an open sky or in cheap, rough posadas. For a year he travels through Spain, from Vigo in the north to the south coast, where he is trapped by the outbreak of the Spanish Civil War.

Lee's lyrical account of his voyages is considered a masterpiece of English travel writing. Experiencing a Spain

Top: goblets made by Roger in 1972 during his time at Ealing in west London. He fired his pots in a cross-draft kiln assembled from storage heater bricks. The same goblets were shown to Mick Casson when Roger applied for a place on the Harrow School of Art studio potter's course.

Below: the first kiln was fired with the crudest of home-made burners (1972 vintage), as Roger used his scientific background to find solutions to ceramics challenges

that ranges from squalor to extreme beauty, Lee creates a story capturing the spirit and atmosphere of the towns and countryside he passes through.

This romantic adventure inspired Roger to escape, at least temporarily, the familiar North Devon landscape and seek warmer climes. With a banjo on his knee, rather than a violin under his chin, Roger decided to recreate Lee's journey through Spain, but then moved on to Morocco where he was charmed by the place and the people. He was to return a few years later, after he had begun experimenting with ceramics, and attempt to throw some pots Moroccan-style.

Travel, postgraduate research and "a slide sideways into teaching" were to bridge the gap between education and a new life in the potter's studio. Roger's teaching activities

Class reunion in 2011 from Roger's years on the studio pottery course at Harrow from 1973 to 1975.

"Harrow changed my life," he says. "The teachers were practitioners, with skill and vision, and this was what they passed on to us." Roger and the other students were pushed hard, cramming three years of work into the two-year course.

indirectly provided his first exposure to the joys of ceramics and therefore changed his life forever.

Early teaching, alongside research projects, turned into a more formal tutorial role at Ickenham Grammer School in the London suburb of Ruislip. His sixth-formers would bring their lunch to the lab, hanging around the equipment and aquariums.

One student disappeared mysteriously and repeatedly during the lunch breaks. Roger's curiosity was piqued, and one day he followed the pupil. Having left the academic sanctity of the science block behind, the student entered the school's pottery studio, where he spent a happy hour conjuring up creations from clay. Something clicked. Roger began to get his hands dirty and has never looked back.

Heading for Harrow

At this stage, there were no plans for a career in ceramics. Roger had moved from Devon to West London, where there were marine research and teaching opportunities. Leaving an earlier temporary home in Shepherd's Bush, he relocated to a rented house in Ealing, where he established an entirely amateur pottery workshop in the lavatory. Here he began the prolonged process of metamorphosis from scientist to artist – and from teacher back to pupil.

Even as an amateur, Roger wasn't averse to reckless experimentation and extensive risk-taking in his pottery endeavours. On advice from a friend, he had bought a Rayefco wheel and was using wood ash from the grate during the firing process. He fired his pots in a cross-draft kiln assembled from storage heater bricks in the back garden. To pre-heat the kiln, he attached one end of a garden hose to

A student
piece from
Roger's time
at Harrow,
bringing
together his
newfound
expertise in
throwing,
decorating,
glazing and
firing

Roger's father found him a house just north of Barnstaple, at Muddiford. Roger set up a small studio next to the even smaller cottage and confronted the challenges of building a kiln, establishing a business and supporting a family.

the gas tap in the kitchen and the other to a gas poker about 25 yards away in the firebox.

The first kiln was fired with the crudest of burners. Roger had flattened the nozzle of an old cylinder vacuum cleaner attachment, then wired it to a length of copper pipe leading to a long run of 'home brew' plastic tubing and a 10 gallon drum of paraffin set on the garden wall. The copper pipe dripped paraffin into the jet of the burner. It worked surprisingly well, demonstrating the marriage of science and creativity that is needed to set up and run a successful pottery. Quite literally, Roger was playing with fire.

There were plenty of failures during this period of part-time potting,

Roger Cockram stoneware lidded jar with incised decoration and semi-glazed finish, c.1979

To this day, Roger has 'once-fired' every pot he has made, whether earthenware, stoneware or even porcelain

but he built up enthusiasm and confidence, producing a large number of pieces, some of which showed promise. None were offered for sale, but simply stashed away for future reference. Steadfastly self-taught, Roger could have continued in this vein for years but for a series of events that was to trigger a permanent change in direction.

In no particular order, Roger got married to Judy, discovered the existence of a production pottery course at Harrow School of Art, and saw his marine research funding dry up. It was clearly decision time. The Harrow course

From Northcott Farm in the early 1980s, a large incised stoneware cider jar and tankard - forming part of Roger's standard range at the time.

He mixed the clay in an old bath by treading it with his bare feet. He was using the local Devon ball clay, mixed with a clay-bearing sand from St Agnes in Cornwall, the same source he uses today.

*Part-glazed
Roger Cockram
lidded jar,
c.1981,
with incised
decoration.
Between 1976
and 1985,
Roger's output
was largely
domestic wares,
made using his
own clay recipe.*

seemed to offer everything the aspiring potter needed to move from amateur to professional, and Roger applied to join the 1973 intake.

It was a good time to become a professional potter. Founding fathers Bernard Leach and Michael Cardew were still on the scene, preaching the gospel of handmade, functional and affordable ceramics for the masses. In the other corner, Hans Coper was at a highly creative stage of his health-blighted career, while soulmate and mentor Lucy Rie was still ploughing her 'modernist' furrow.

Not only was there strong demand for British handmade tableware, but studio pottery was gaining credibility and desirability as a recognised form of visual art. The British art school movement had reached its zenith, with ample government funding available and a commitment by the state to encourage creativity in virtually every field. Rejecting the traditionalist teachings of Leach and Cardew, and also eschewing the modernist methods of Coper and Rie, was a third group of so-called post-modern ceramicists, turned on by the cultural highs of the 1960s. Their rather academic and generally non-functional creations owed little to the potter's wheel and 'old-fashioned' media such as stoneware.

It is perhaps a credit to Roger that he avoided the trendy field of 'new ceramics' and instead set his sights on being a more

traditional craft potter. Being somewhat older (at 26) than many of the typical art school students, he was seeking a lasting career making and selling pots, rather than an opportunity simply to play with clay.

Harrow School of Art had, in 1963, attempted to establish a full-time and vocational diploma course for production potters. While the School failed to meet the stringent demands of the National Diploma in Art & Design system, it persisted with the concept of furnishing students with all the tools necessary to begin commercial design and production of ceramics.

The revised approach, although lacking in the desired full certification, resulted in the Harrow Studio Pottery

Roger built a new 90 cubic feet catenary arch kiln in one of the barns, intending to construct a chimney up through the roof. Given the height of the building and lack of money for scaffolding, he borrowed empty oil drums to stand on and laid bricks around himself, building the chimney from the inside.

Course, which was a highly intensive two-year programme of practical and theoretical tuition. The course aimed to offer a vocational rather than an academic education to help meet the growing needs of students wanting a sound, practical training before setting up their own workshop.

It was immediately successful, delivering a steady stream of ceramics talent that underpinned the 'new wave' of potters still working today. In 1990, the Bachelor of Arts Ceramics Course (now defunct) emerged from the original Harrow Studio Pottery programme, provided by the University of Westminster.

Heading up the ceramics department at Harrow from 1963 were Mick Casson and (Professor) Victor Margrie. These highly successful proponents of the potter's art were to have huge and lasting influence over their charges. They initiated the new studio pottery course, and oversaw what was arguably its most productive period.

Neither founder of the course had complete expertise in commercial-scale pottery production, or some of the

emerging modernist/post-modernist techniques, so they enlisted the help of several other gifted ceramicists to expand the coverage of the programme and provide a broad education in a variety of methods.

With an intention to teach practical, professional skills rather than take the traditional art school approach of focusing on ideas, Colin Pearson, a professional potter who had trained in workshops rather than art school, was recruited to teach repetition throwing. Pearson, having worked at Winchcombe Pottery with Ray Finch and at Aylesford Pottery with David Leach, was a highly accomplished thrower as well as a sensitive maker.

Earlier students such as Walter Keeler and Janice Tchalenko were to return regularly and share their experiences and expertise, while more maverick potters such as sculptural specialist Mo Jupp joined industry stalwarts such as Pearson in disseminating their ideas, knowledge and skills.

Roger Cockram may have missed the first wave or two of Harrow productivity, but his arrival at the School in 1973

was still timely and exposed him to a remarkable roster of teaching talent that helped shape his future.

The magic of Mick Casson

Margrie had, by this time, been appointed director of the newly formed Crafts Advisory Committee (later the Crafts Council), leaving Casson in sole charge of the course for the first time – a period he later described as the worst 18 months of his life! In spite of faculty politics and spirit-sapping administrative chores, he maintained his rapport with the students, many of whom dubbed the period a "golden age".

Roger shares that view. He appears to have been the last student chosen by Casson for the course. Joining in September 1973, Roger recalls that Casson had "one good year" left at Harrow, and made sure it was packed full of workshop-style training within an aesthetic and philosophical context. Guest tutors such as Pearson and Russell Collins were to prove inspirational and educational, while Casson himself was to return as a guest tutor after he had left the School.

The interview itself was a revelation. In Roger's words, "I turned up with boxes full of pots, including some Coper-like goblets from my Ealing kiln and lots of drawings, some of which I had produced as a scientist. I started by showing just the drawings. Mick leafed through my folder, then asked if I had any pots with me."

Taking the department head outside, Roger was hugely impressed as Casson sat on the ground, hauling pots from tea chests. After the hierarchy and bureaucracy of science and academia, it was a welcome surprise to see 'management' getting their hands dirty.

"He looked at my goblets and said, 'Don't worry, we'll teach you how to throw'!". Roger insists that the goblets were actually "pretty good", but he was delighted to be accepted for the course, although he discovered later that he would have to pay his way as funding had been withdrawn.

Mick Casson's CV shows why Roger and so many others left Harrow with such enthusiasm for their new-found art and profession. He had made his first pots at an evening

Stoneware storage pots, which formed part of Roger's standard output in the early 1980s. He intended initially to continue the local tradition and make English slipwares, fired at relatively low temperatures using the red North Devon clay. In order to achieve greater durability, he switched to the denser and stronger stoneware.

At Northcott Farm in the early 1980s, Roger had been experimenting with some small porcelain bowls and bottles designed to catch ash from the wood-fired kiln. These began to sell quite well in smart little galleries that would never have touched his tankards, casseroles, pitchers and bread crocks.

class in 1945. Art and craft studies at Shoreditch College led to a teacher's course specialising in art and woodwork which, in turn, steered him to an art teacher's diploma at Hornsey School of Arts and Crafts in 1948. Fellow student potters included his future wife Sheila Wilmot and Victor Margrie.

In 1952, Casson established a pottery in the basement of his uncle's hardware shop in Bloomsbury. Using red clay, black slip and a richly reactive lead-based tin glaze, he produced useful and decorative wares, including a memorable series of lidded jars with modelled knobs in the form of abstracted birds that were shown at the Arts and Crafts Exhibition Society's 1957 open exhibition at the Victoria and Albert (V&A) Museum.

Casson then taught evening classes at West London's Harrow School of Art, where Margrie had become head of the ceramics department. Casson taught for a time on the School's national diploma in design course. This ultimately resulted in him joining Margrie to set up the full-time Studio Pottery Course in 1963.

A founder member of the Craftsmen Potters Association – now the Craft Potters Association (CPA) – Casson conducted and coordinated countless workshops and demonstrations, reaching his largest audience in 1976 with his BBC-TV series *The Craft Of The Potter*. He served as a member, and as vice chairman (1986-88), of the Crafts Council, and participated in its craftsman's tours. Casson died in 2003 at the age of 78. With his art school

31

Top: these bowls were produced in the wood-firing kiln at Northcott. Here Roger was experimenting with glaze-trailing, instead of the more traditional slip-trailing form of decoration.

Below: incised wood-fired stoneware pitchers from 1986. These were all about the great Devon tradition of robust pitchers carried to the fields for farm workers, either filled with water or cider.

background, Casson confessed to learning as much as the students from the other members of staff at Harrow, influencing greatly his own approach to throwing. Harrow had inaugurated an experimental kiln site where students could build their own kiln and experiment with a range of firings. Again, Casson felt this facility changed his own ideas about the possibilities of clay and firing.

Roger has very fond memories of his time at Harrow,

particularly when Casson was still at the helm. "Harrow changed my life. The teachers were practitioners, with skill and vision, and this was what they passed on to us." Roger and the other students were pushed hard, cramming three years of work into the two-year course. Standards were high, and Casson was demanding.

During the Harrow years, Roger describes himself as "visually illiterate". "I had no equipment then to view things the way I do now." However, he felt he had the rest of his life to learn how to be creative. For the moment, he wanted to learn how to make and to *do*. "It was obvious to me that I could make a living from pots, and I was determined to do it."

Every aspect of his future craft was on show and available to learn and practise at Harrow, enabling Roger to gain an essential understanding of clays, glazes, kiln construction and operation, plus all manner of throwing, shaping, modelling and decorating techniques.

It was very much a vocational course. First, students were taught to make clay cylinder after cylinder. The tutor would then come and squash down all but the best. This taught

repetition and consistency, essential in production pottery.

The quest for perfection also began at Harrow, as the tutors pushed the students ever harder to deliver pots of an increasingly high standard. While Roger was joining clay for throwing a neck on to a large bottle form, Casson chided him, "What do you mean nobody will know if it's on the inside? You'll know!"

There was a similar approach to making jug forms, then challenges to produce more demanding items such as teapots. Roger already had firm ideas about what type of pottery he wanted to make, and drew the line at a traditional, cane-handled, oriental-style teapot,

The bowls opposite led gradually to more detailed, figurative pieces

inspired by rock pools and gullies on the North Devon coast, such as the piece shown above. This 1988 bowl is considered a 'signpost' towards Roger's future direction and the figurative work that was to follow.

making his with the conventional 'British' handle opposite the spout. "I clearly wasn't in the Leach tradition. Why should I make a teapot with a bamboo handle? It meant nothing to me!" Being somewhat older then some of the other students, Roger was able to take the occasional stand against certain aspects of the teaching programme.

However, he was completely at one with the School's

Roger moved to his current site at Chittlehampton in 1986, living initially in neighbouring Victoria House (right) while he converted a barn into the pottery

ethos. "The idea was to teach us how to set up as studio potters. At the time there was a real dearth of craftspeople. Like me, a lot of those on the course came from other fields. We were aware that it was an opportunity touched with gold. We were knocking at the door first thing in the morning and we worked as late as we could."

One night at Harrow, Roger was firing an oil kiln at the experimental site. Around one o'clock in the morning, he opened the spy hole and a jet of flame shot out. Somebody looking out of nearby Northwick Park Hospital saw the flame and called the fire brigade. Roger was also using the heat of the kiln to make a late supper. To his relief, the attending firemen were quite relaxed about the entire incident, and settled down with a cup of tea to hear all about Roger's experiences and experiments.

Other Harrow memories centre around selling pots along

London's Bayswater Road and at Green Park on a Sunday, competing for the best spots along the railings opposite the Underground station entrance. "Thanks to these sales, I managed to eat while at college," says Roger.

"It was a sort of crazy compressed apprenticeship," he recalls, "with very long hours and the steepest learning curve of my life." As for the guest teachers, who came in for a day or two each week, Roger remembers Casson himself, sculptural potter Mo Jupp, Walter Keeler, Russell Collins and "the inspirational" Colin Pearson.

When he died in 2007, aged 84, Pearson's obituary in *The Guardian* newspaper described him as "one of the most creatively charismatic of postwar British potters". David Whiting, who wrote the obituary, called him "a masterly educator who imparted his love of clay and his extraordinary knowledge of the chemistry of ceramics to generations of students".

Roger recalls a conversation with Pearson. "Well, Roger, you've learnt to biscuit-fire and glaze. Now I'll show you how to avoid doing so." To this day, Roger has 'once-fired' every pot he has made, whether earthenware, stoneware or even porcelain.

Biscuit-firing is the first of two separate periods in the kiln used in the production of glazed pottery since medieval times. The extremely common process is used in order to

make the work strong enough to handle when applying glazes. Once-firing is a still more ancient method, seen by some as more risky, but saving the potter time, energy, double-handling of the pieces – and resulting in a different reaction between glaze and clay.

The original objective of the Harrow course was to create production potters. They, presumably, would in turn establish their own potteries and hire apprentices to continue the process. More than 800 students benefited from a Harrow ceramics education.

However, not all students were willing to take the same path, and their interpretation of 'functional' ceramics can vary enormously. Keeler, for example, turned his back on conventional forms of domestic pottery, thus ignoring the doctrine of Leach, Cardew and the other founding fathers. He moved 'off-piste' to use his new salt-glaze kiln for more striking and elaborate pieces.

During his long career, his work has ranged from stoneware and raku to earthenware. His early interest in sculptural pieces was replaced gradually by a commitment to functional pots. These, however, are seldom orthodox in design and appearance, having a strong ornamental element with unexpected and pleasing details. They bridge the gap between practical domestic pottery and the more collector-orientated art pieces.

Russell Collins began producing hand-thrown pots at Hook Norton Pottery on the edge of the Cotswolds after leaving the Harrow course

From around 2005, a tall spiral vase capturing the movement of fish rising through the water

and establishing his workshop in 1969. While individual pieces form a small part of his repertoire, Collins has stayed true to functional domestic items and attractive stoneware for the catering industry.

Former Harrow student Janice Tchalenko, from the class of '69, also stuck closely to the functional pottery path, carving out a niche as an innovative high-volume tableware designer. She began her professional pottery career making functional stoneware within the Leach/Cardew tradition. In the late 1970s she began experimenting with decoration using free forms and colourful patterns. Her subsequent work at Dartington Pottery is greatly admired, where she produced tableware with brightly painted surface decoration.

Jane Hamlyn, on the Harrow course in 1972, went on to specialise in salt-glazed stoneware. Her work is thrown and hand-built, often highly decorated, and not always

*'P****d as a Newt' teapot, c.2005. Roger's approach to the humble teapot is to try and make people smile!*

Detail of
a seahorse,
a Cockram
favourite, on
a tall, flared
stoneware
vase, c.2005

functional – although she claims to make pots both for use and for show. Like Keeler, she likes her functional pieces to provoke a reaction.

Roger himself, during his long career as a studio potter, has veered from the purely functional to the exclusively decorative, but has ultimately found a way to accommodate both.

Cottage industry

Immediately after leaving the Harrow course, Roger took his wife Judy back to his home turf of North Devon in order to start a life in the pottery trade. His father found him a house just north of Barnstaple, at Muddiford, and life at Dell Cottage began. Roger set up a small studio next to the even smaller cottage and confronted the challenges of building a kiln, establishing a business, and supporting a family.

He intended initially to continue the local ceramics tradition and make English slipwares, fired at relatively low temperatures using the red North Devon clay. In order to achieve greater durability of his pots, he switched to the denser and stronger stoneware, but continued to slip-trail for decoration.

According to the strict definition, stoneware is dense, impermeable and hard enough to resist scratching by a steel point. It differs from porcelain because it is more opaque, and normally only partially vitrified. Stoneware may be vitreous or semi-vitreous and is usually coloured grey or brownish because of impurities

in the clay. It is normally glazed and generally once-fired.

Given that stoneware requires higher firing temperatures than earthenware, Roger needed the right kiln for the job. He first built a catenary arch kiln, fired by burning wood. Once complete, this type of kiln is self-supporting. The arch itself is an inverted replica of the curve produced when a heavy rope is hung from two points on the same horizontal plane. Such kilns can often be very attractive, given the graceful form.

Roger remembers firing it on 29 May 1976 – the hottest day of the century thus far. "It was so hot I was down to my swimming trunks!" The kiln was at first so badly insulated that, by the end of the firing, it would glow gently. He claims beautiful effects from the wood firing, as well as great satisfaction from the effects of the fire on his inherent pyromania.

Given that the mid-1970s were the days of brown kitchens and still browner pots, Roger was making casseroles, bread crocks, Devonshire pitchers and tankards, all once-fired in homage to Colin Pearson. He mixed the clay in an old bath by treading it with his bare feet. He was using the local Devon ball clay (described earlier) mixed with a

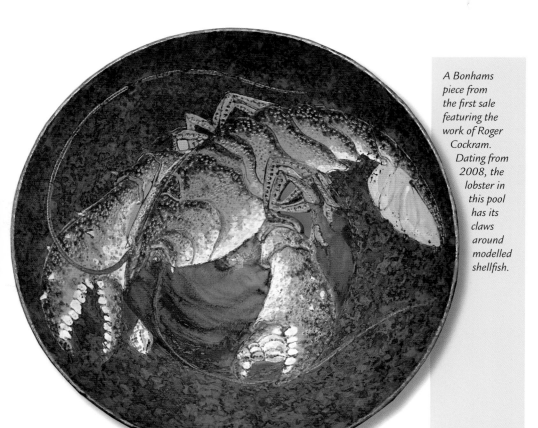

clay-bearing sand from St Agnes in Cornwall, the same source he still uses today. "You simply haven't lived until you've trodden wet clay!"

The threat of chilblains from the touch of cold clay on bare feet, coupled with an inability to manipulate the clay once the temperature had plummeted in winter, led Roger to seek a £200 bank loan to buy an old baker's cake mixing machine. The pain was reduced immediately, and the mixer is still in use (as is the bath, but for storing reclaimed clay). The bank debt was repaid as quickly as possible, as Roger had no intention of paying more interest than absolutely necessary.

Creativity and poverty tend to bring out the best in potters. Roger found the bricks for his kiln at the coal-fired power station in East Yelland, on the nearby Taw estuary, which was in the process of closing down because of higher coal costs. Roger tried to scrounge some, but was told he would have to buy them at the price paid originally by the

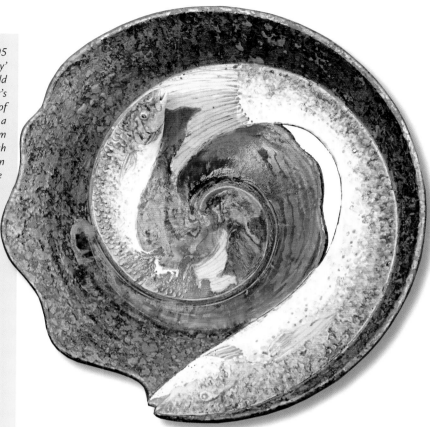

From the 2005 'Art in Clay' show at Hatfield House, Roger's depiction of salmon in a pool came from watching the fish in the autumn just before they leapt up a fall and continued their journey

plant's owner. Fortunately, the power station's index card system showed that the bricks dated from 1936, so the price was very reasonable and Roger had his cut-price kiln. The remainder of the brick haul can be found today outside his current workshop.

The kiln was fired with softwood off-cuts from a local sawmill and, due to rather inadequate fireboxes, had a tendency to choke up by about cone 10. (For ceramics production, kilns are fired not just to a temperature but to a 'cone' level, which accounts for time as well as temperature. Cone 10 has a melting point of approximately 1,280°C.)

Ingenious as ever – that science again! –Roger hit on the idea of blowing air into the ash in the fireboxes using some old Harrow oil burners that he had made at college. This worked quite well in spreading the ash into the kiln. Worried about the cold air being blown, he decided to turn on the oil as well. Cone 11 was thus achieved, and

he was to use this same procedure for the next 10 years. (For the uninitiated, stoneware and porcelain need high firing temperatures, between cone 8 and cone 14, which results in greater density of the finished piece and superior strength.)

Roger and Judy lived at Muddiford for three years, representing a period of rather cramped potting mixed in with some part-time teaching. Their first daughter, Josie, was born while they lived at the tiny cottage. However, the next move involved a bigger house, larger workshop and an enlarged family.

Down on the farm

The Cockrams' new home was Higher Northcott Farm at Cullompton, an ancient pile of outbuildings and a thatched Devon farmhouse that needed a new roof. There was plenty of space for the pottery and to store the firewood for the kiln, but the farm was so remote that no one could find it.

Roger built a new 90 cubic feet catenary arch kiln in one of the barns, intending to construct a chimney up through

the roof. Given the height of the building and lack of money for scaffolding, he borrowed empty oil drums, stood on them and laid bricks around him, building the chimney from the inside.

Between 1976 and 1985, Roger's output was largely

domestic wares, made using his own clay recipe mixed in the aforementioned baker's machine. He had a short list of regular buyers, but was about to find himself in a rather precarious situation because of the relative isolation of the new pottery and the chill winds of change blowing down from the Palace of Westminster.

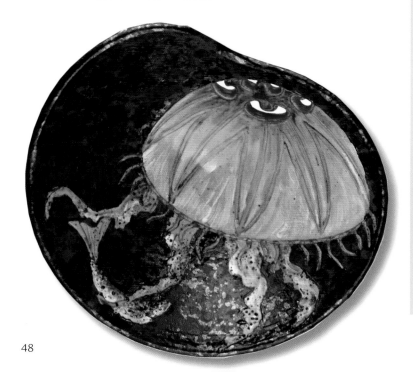

Retail sales suffered from the lack of passing trade, forcing Roger into "dreadful" cold-selling trips around the country with tatty boxes of pots being thrust upon reluctant gallery owners by a self-confessed "grubby" potter.
This was another steep learning curve, with the challenge made worse by the arrival of the 1980s and recession.

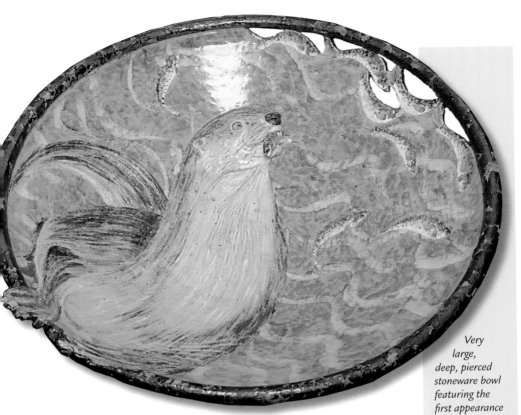

Potters throughout the land found that the market for domestic ware had virtually dried up. In Roger's case, he had been experimenting with some small porcelain bowls and bottles designed to catch ash from the wood-fired kiln. These began to sell quite well in smart little galleries that would never have touched the tankards, casseroles, pitchers and bread crocks. "The porcelain kept us going," recalls Roger, "along with the occasional large cider jar."

"In the early days, I would drive into the middle of Soho with a car full of pots. I would simply walk into a gallery and ask if they wanted to buy anything. It was absolutely hopeless. Gradually I discovered shows. I also had a little showroom at the farm, and sent images to galleries instead of walking in cold. I had to learn about being a businessman and salesman. I also started approaching fine art galleries and selling little bits of individual ware."

Thanks to the experimentation with porcelain, Roger still had something to sell – and he has been reluctant ever since to place all of his eggs in one basket (or stoneware pot!). He continues to try out new glazes, forms, sizes and

decoration, so will hopefully always have something new
to offer a fickle public.

Rock pool epiphany

For many reasons, the 1980s wasn't to be the happiest
of decades for the Cockram family. While juggling
the demands of a time-consuming pottery, some sheep,
a few bees and three children (Josie had been joined by
Martha and Lucy), Roger's marriage failed. Another
move therefore became necessary, this time to his current
location at Chittlehampton.

The new site, up on the hills above the village, has
panoramic views of the sheep-studded fields, distant
farmhouses and old stone walls. The wind-swept house was
home for several years, while the once open-fronted barn is
still Roger's workshop and gallery.

Roger threw himself into converting the existing
buildings into his perfect pottery, enclosing the barn
to create a large workshop, home for the kilns and a
showroom for his finished wares. His giant topiary jug out
front not only advertises the potter's craft but also conceals
a large and unsightly water tank that supplies the pottery.

His arrival on the outskirts of the village aroused plenty

of curiosity and suspicion among the Chittlehampton locals, particularly when a succession of young men and women joined him to help out in the studio. Once he had established his credentials as a bona fide Barnstaple lad earning a crust by making pots, he was accepted by the community – and is now at the heart of it.

Chittlehampton was built originally around an open

Opposite:
Roger with one of his biggest, most challenging and most expensive pots to date, shown at a much earlier stage on the previous page

Above right: a smaller pierced fish globe produced for the 2009 'Art in Clay' show at Hatfield House

Overleaf:
Roger working on a striking teapot design, c.2009

square, with a particularly fine church (St Hieritha) on one side. It was one of the early villages in the Saxon occupation, c.700 in date, and there were once reputedly eight alehouses in the village. Today, The Bell is all that remains, serving a population of around 800 – half the level recorded in 1801. The Bell has been in The Square since 1888, and has been run by the same family for the past 30 years.

Chittlehampton is around 20 miles from the north coast above Barnstaple, and during the sobering days following the 1986 marriage break-up Roger found himself exploring the rugged coastline of his youth, losing himself amid the rocky outcrops and shallow pools that teemed with marine life. These walks led to the next phase of his career, as he learnt to combine a love of the environment with a passion for pots.

His regular beat became the surf beaches at Saunton

Sands and
Croyde, and
the sandstone
rocks and brackish
pools of Baggy Point – a
headland that separates
Croyde Bay and Morte Bay.
Outside of the summer tourist season, this is an area
of great beauty and isolation, with winter storms creating a
spectacular land- and seascape.

A particular incident was responsible for this pottery
epiphany. While sitting reading the Sunday paper on the
beach at Down End, Croyde, Roger became aware that
his three daughters were, unusually, making no noise.
Alarmed, he set off to investigate, only to find them
peering into a rock pool, watching the marine life trapped
by the departing tide.

In an instant, he realised that he could incorporate
this vision into his pots. It had woken him up to a new
possibility, where his scientific background could play a
role in his work as a potter.

Thanks to his original education in marine ecology,
Roger was in a perhaps unique position to interpret what
he was seeing along the Devon coast in the form of pottery.
Having rediscovered a fascination with the natural
world, particularly the sea, he seized the opportunity
to create a new breed of decorative ceramics, while

continuing to produce more traditional domestic wares.

It would have been easy to have simply added fishy themes to his work, following a long tradition in art pottery of incorporating shell designs, modelled fish forms and patterns of scales or waves. This didn't appeal. Neither did the production in clay of detailed recreations of marine beasts.

Roger was instead captivated by the movement of water, and by the relationship of creatures with their environment. All that he saw when peering into a rock pool had to be recreated in clay, including water, rocks, light and shade. This required more experimentation with glazes, clays, textures, decorating techniques and patterns.

"I started painting from the pools for the first time, and on the pots too. I worked up lots of new glazes and

Top: a spectacular Pufferfish teapot, created for the 2009 Bonhams sale in London's New Bond Street

Below: a delicate porcelain pot with modelled fish lid from around 2006

vitreous slips and started applying them in different ways – sponging and stippling, etc. This was with an eye to catch moments I had seen or situations I could observe and distill into something that worked as a pot."

Another new influence was Roger's second wife, Ros. Born in Staffordshire and attending the then Loughborough College of Art and Design, Ros had trained originally as a textiles designer, but had always loved painting. By way of London and Dorset, she had found her way to Devon and encountered Roger at a craft show. She became an enthusiastic supporter of Roger's new artistic direction, urging more drawings, the use of additional colours, and the creation of larger pots. "For the last 20 or so years I just couldn't have done what I have been able to do without the help of Ros," says

Roger adds incised decoration to one of his taller vase designs, produced in 2011. Focusing on watery themes, he needs the depth of the pot to show the transition from the inky darkness of the deep to the light near the surface of the sea.

Roger. "She not only runs all the day-to-day business side of things, but is an excellent and supportive critic for ideas – and helps in the studio in many, many ways."

Ros is a versatile artist, with a painter's eye for colour and a flair for design. Her own work often features highly detailed floral studies in bold colours, helping her to inspire Roger to break out of his 'comfort zone' and traditional palette. Ros Cockram's paintings now share the exhibition space at the pottery.

While Roger bears the brunt of the decoration, Ros will often abandon her own work at the easel or in the home to help in the painstaking process of applying layers of 'undercoat'. He can then take the greater glory by painting the more visible elements in the final stage of decoration before the piece enters the kiln for firing.

"A lot of what I do is still about visiting the coast and

the rock pools and gullies at Baggy Point, but also about memory," says Roger. "I'm also trying to capture more nebulous things – the power of the sea, the unstoppability of it. It is all about capturing that moment."

Early efforts saw water and light effects swirled inside conventional bowl forms, or painted two-dimensional depictions of rock pool life. These were soon to make way for more ambitious and effective interpretations.

When arriving at Chittlehampton, the intention was to continue wood firing his kiln with supplies from a nearby sawmill. When it closed, just as the pottery was ready, cylinder gas was brought in to act as a substitute. Given the nature of the new, more demanding, work, the consistency

of the gas-fired kiln proved useful, and a mains gas supply was later secured both for the pottery site and for the Cockrams' village home.

Roger does not believe that a potter should begin working on a piece without first knowing what is to be achieved, both in terms of form and decoration. "When a good pot works, there is a reason for every element. There is a conceptual marriage between form and surface. I want pieces to have power and stillness, but not to shout louder than what's on the surface. In the case of a bowl with a salmon swimming around it, the form has come about because of the circle I saw the fish making."

Roger believes it is "wrong" to make a shape and then decide what to put on it. "Both have to go together." When a student asks him, "What should I do now?", Roger will reply, "The answer is behind you". Roughly translated as,

"You should have known where you were going before you started the journey".

The first time that Roger tried making his trademark swirling bowls with the head of a fish protruding, it simply fell off. He had modelled the head in the same clay as the body, and that didn't work. This called for a different clay recipe and more experimentation. "All along the way there have been lots of tests. It's a question of trial and error but always with an intention in mind. I'm always after a particular effect."

From the rearing fish trying to escape the gullies and pools, Roger moved on to frogs climbing out of the garden pond at his new home in Chittlehampton village. He also began to reproduce shells and shellfish, incorporate lobsters and crabs, then seahorses, jellyfish and octopi.

The work became increasingly figurative, attracting

Top: detail of a 2011 Bonhams piece featuring parrots on a wall-mounted shallow dish

Below: kiln opening at the 2006 Collectors' Day

One of a pair
of calling bird
bottles made
for the 2011
Bonhams sale

new interest from galleries and collectors, while no doubt alarming Roger's more traditional pottery contemporaries who dwell in a world of more functional forms.

"With the figurative pieces, there's no end function in mind," he admits. This philosophy lifts the boundaries and allows Roger to create extraordinary bowls, bottles, globes, jugs and flasks that have little in common with domestic tableware.

Roger's decoration features the natural hues of the sea and the slippery or scaly bodies of the creatures that live in it, with startling flashes of colour. His work centres on ideas derived from observations of water. Its movement, rhythms and colours are a major preoccupation, and he strives to capture the impressions of movement and depth in his vessels.

"My use of fish, for example, springs from the fact that they cannot help but show movement. This helps enormously to keep a sense of rhythm going in the piece I'm working on."

Having tried to catch a moment or situation, such as a fish shooting up a gully in the rocks after a storm, Roger usually produces a number of rough drawings that help translate the concept into a pot.

All of the work is hand thrown and then modified to capture elements of movement. This can result in spirals of fish

'swimming' or the head of a fish emerging from the surface of foaming water.

Larger pots will often be made as two parts, joined later in a nerve-wracking process that requires just enough rigidity for the bottom to bear the weight of the top. The pot continues to be worked on the wheel as the join is concealed and strengthened both inside and out.

These procedures take place at different stages during the drying of the pot. The finished piece is then set aside to dry completely before the, often lengthy, process of decoration begins.

Roger has developed a series of special glazes in his

Top: three 2011 pots drying out and waiting for decoration

Below: from the 2012 range of pots, the interior decoration of a deep-sided bowl inspired by the movement of water off the North Devon coast

studio. A large number of different formulations, often up to a dozen, are used to build up the tones on subjects such as salmon. The glazes are generally painted on to the form with a 'Pointillist', or dotted, technique, using several layers.

Opposite: fish still make an appearance in 2012, albeit in a more 'impressionist' way, on the new range of pots, here lined up by the kiln ready for their big day

The background to many of the pieces produced from the 1990s is often a mottled pewter colour that suggests a sense of depth such as that observed by Roger when diving or watching the sea from Devon clifftops. This effect is produced by using sponged layers of several vitreous slips that melt only partially during firing and to varying extents, thus creating the impression of depth.

The process is highly elaborate and time-consuming. Over the course of several weeks, Roger will assemble a

Bond Street. Few living potters have the honour of seeing their work incorporated into sales featuring the great and the good of British ceramics.

The relationship with Bonhams is owed largely to ceramics guru Richard Dennis (who, in the 2006 New Year's Honours List, was awarded an OBE for services to the Staffordshire pottery industry) and partly to an Essex-based art pottery dealer named Nick Garner.

Roger had first encountered Richard in 1987 at the annual Spring Fair held in Birmingham's National Exhibition Centre. Throughout his life, Richard has not only collected pots on an epic scale but has also encouraged and promoted many potters. He introduced himself to Roger, offered him the chance of a private show at the Dennis-run gallery on Kensington High Street in London, and even offered

support while Roger produced work for the exhibition.

Given that Richard's tastes embrace pottery by established and emerging designers from the Arts and Crafts, Art Nouveau and Art Deco periods through to the modern day, Roger was joining some remarkable company, ranging from Pugin and William De Morgan, through the Martin Brothers and William Moorcroft, to Bernard Moore and (Sir) Edward Elton.

Having thus become part of the Dennis 'collection', Roger was about to see his work move to a still bigger stage. Phillips auctioneers had, in 1999, staged the first-ever auction of works by ceramics designer Sally Tuffin for Dennis Chinaworks – created by her and her husband, one Richard Dennis. Given the success of this and subsequent sales, Bonhams (which in 2001 had merged with Phillips) decided to continue the tradition. At this point, Sally was the only living British ceramics designer to have her own annual sale at a major auction house.

From early 2012, a particularly tall and slender pitcher with fish handle and extended spout

Enter the scene Nick Garner. This entertaining character, a former rock band roadie, had been championing the cause of Roger Cockram for some time. While touring the antiques and collectables fairs of England, he had been selling pots by both Dennis Chinaworks and Roger. He began to lobby Mark Oliver, Director of 20th Century Decorative Arts at Bonhams, to consider a Roger Cockram sale.

In 2008, a special event, 'Richard Dennis – A Potted History', was organised by Bonhams and curated by Richard himself. As well as featuring part of Richard's own vast and important collection, the sale was to feature 'guest' potters invited by Richard. Thanks to the efforts of both Nick and Richard, one of these star turns was Roger. Others included Grahame Clarke, Laurence McGowan, Jonathan Chiswell Jones and Maureen Minchin.

The event introduced Roger's work to a new audience and was to raise his profile in collecting circles. On offer in March 2008 were 10 lots showcasing the best of Roger's highly individual pottery style.

There was considerable interest in the event, with the top-floor saleroom filled to capacity by the time the work of the contemporary designers came under Mark Oliver's hammer.

Representatives of US and European buyers

81

meant that UK collectors had tough competition. Prices in general soared above the Bonhams' estimates. In Roger's case, two pieces reached £1,700 (before buyer's premium): a 'Rising Salmon' 57cm wide stoneware bowl; and 'Shoal of Fish', a 36cm high rounded, pierced, footed vessel depicting a shoal of tropical fish circling the pot – the estimate had been just £500-£600. The sale of all 10 pieces grossed almost £9,500 after buyer's commission, which

The beach at Croyde with its rocky outcrops, pools and gullies. The North Devon coastline and its natural wonders

wasn't bad for a banjo-playing biologist from Barnstaple.

September 2009 saw the second Bonhams sale to feature Roger's work. He pushed the boundaries with his 'Puffer Fish' teapot, dabbled with new subjects such as the 57cm high 'Otter with Young' pot and revisited his beloved rock pools with the 33cm wide 'Pool at Croyde' bowl.

A year later, Roger had clearly been experimenting. The 10 pieces offered for sale in 2010 were perhaps the most

challenging to date, not least because the potter had ducked out of his comfort zone, delivering exotic species and producing porcelain instead of stoneware. The less familiar subject matter clearly didn't deter bidders.

Selling at Bonhams in 2010 were 'Marauding Macaws', a 27cm high vase featuring Scarlet Macaws in Roger's 'Tropical Gold' series, and the 37cm tall 'Flowers and Frogs' design, also hand thrown in hard-paste porcelain, this time featuring Hibiscus flowers, Frangipani blooms and two Golden Tree Frogs.

Another ground-breaking design was the 48cm wide 'Emperor Wave' pierced and incised porcelain screen, decorated with Emperor Angelfish, and featuring gilt highlights. An extraordinary teapot made an appearance. The 'Octopus' was made from gilt-highlighted porcelain. Its intriguing form supported remarkable decoration representing the suckers on the creature's tentacles.

The star pot of Roger's September 2011 Bonhams collection was 'Swimming in a Shoal', a 45cm high lidded, pierced stoneware jar featuring a shoal of highly coloured tropical fish and the subtle use of platinum lustre to suggest the light on the surface of the sea. At the time of writing, it was Roger's intention to contribute to the 2012 sale.

While the Bonhams experience hasn't been without its drawbacks, it has allowed Roger to showcase some spectacular pieces and design approaches that could be incorporated elsewhere in his portfolio. Sometimes these initiatives lead to 'an artistic cul-de-sac', where there is nothing technically wrong with the pots, but Roger simply cannot take them forward. Often this reflects cost issues in terms of materials or time taken.

Roger tries to resist commercial pressure and to remain

true to his principles. "If you're not doing something that is 'you', then it doesn't work and people will feel it. I've just got to do what's right for me."

Having said that, domestic wares haven't been forgotten, and Roger still finds his casseroles, mugs and bowls to be useful 'kiln-fillers', as well as consistent sellers. His range of table- and cookware is highly regarded, practical, but still extremely individual. These pieces aren't festooned with fish or frogs, but do make use of the special glazes and firing techniques used on the decorative or figurative pots.

Three different vitreous slips are sponged on for the domestic ware. These bleed up through one another and react, but still don't form a glaze. The overall effect is one of different surfaces and textures, as well as of varying colours.

The pottery is made using carefully designed clay recipes and fired to temperatures in excess of 1,300°C. This makes

Top: *loading the kiln, late April 2012, showing the large surf and fish bottle seen being formed on page 6*

Overleaf: *the pottery and the potter in April 2012*

it fully vitrified stoneware that can be used both in the microwave and conventional oven, as well as in a normal domestic dishwasher. Bernard Leach and Mick Casson would both be delighted.

Making waves

After 20 years developing and honing his techniques for the figurative pieces, Roger has begun to chart a slightly different course. We haven't seen the last of fish, molluscs or crustaceans, but their role in his work is changing.

He is keen not to be pigeon-holed as a modern reincarnation of the late-19th-century Arts and Crafts potter. The extensive influence of nature on his work means that some in the industry are inclined to put him in the 'Artist Potter' box. He feels this to be a slightly derogative categorisation, suggesting a more limited repertoire, skill-set and ideas.

"My only plea to our potting community is that we cherish all potting traditions – rural and industrial, ancient and contemporary. We should look for the person in the work and not be distracted by fashion."

Inspiration continues to flow from the coastline just a few miles from his studio. Roger is thrilled constantly by

Top: *a selection of smaller 2012 porcelain pieces*

Below: *large stoneware sea surf bottle with fish, shown at an early production stage on page 6*

the power of wind and waves; by the ever-changing patterns of light and shade; and by the movement of the sea itself. This is being reflected in a somewhat more impressionistic approach, where fish are used in a much more subtle way.

"My most recent interest is in the water itself. I have made some quite large jars and bowl forms with spirals thrown deeply into the form when wet on the wheel. There is nothing figurative here, just frozen movement.

"I keep going back to what's out there – the natural world. It might be our

garden pond, the surf at Saunton in winter or the river
at Umberleigh."

Porcelain is back on the menu. Roger is enjoying the effects
of his decoration on the thinner, more delicate pots, bowls
and jars. The discreet use of platinum or gold lustre to capture
sunlight on water provides a jewel-like quality to the smaller
pieces. To achieve this, he has to re-fire the pots to 780°C.

"Glazes are what I have experimented with most. To try and
soften my effects, I start with the glazes I already have. I'll
either try and fire at higher temperatures or modify glazes
to get a softer interaction. Over the past 12 months, there
has been a whole series of tests modifying glazes, resulting
in a freer effect."

For the new bowls, Roger glazes inside when the clay is
damp, but glazes the outside when it's bone dry. This

applies both to stoneware and to porcelain. Vitreous slips are added to the base glaze in the bottom of pots, helping create the illusion of depth.

Roger has also been experimenting with matt glazes, "trying to recreate the darkness at the bottom of the sea when I'm diving, with the lightness towards the top".

Looking back at 40 years of throwing, decorating, glazing and firing, Roger sees it as a journey of discovery. At Harrow, he was pushed to make Leach-style pots inspired by the East. He changed to more traditional English techniques with slip trailing, becoming the 'craftsman potter'.

Domestic stoneware gave way to the nature-influenced studio pottery of the 1990s, leading to the Arts and Crafts

label that has refused to stick. More modelling, more piercing and more figurative work was the main thrust of the last decade, with the Bonhams auction exposure providing a valuable boost.

The latest evolution isn't a change of direction, just another bend in the road, as Roger plots his route through the rest of the decade. There are still plans for a new kiln (with a trolley this time, to spare his 'potter's back'), plenty of shows to attend, lectures to give, demonstrations to arrange, gigs to play and lots more pots to make.

Through his fellowship of the CPA, and full membership of the Devon Guild of Craftsmen, Roger can now be considered part of the ceramics industry 'establishment', but without the negative connotations the term implies. This allows him to share his not inconsiderable experience with those new to the trade, helping him repay the favours

done by Casson and Pearson at Harrow in the early 1970s.

It is a very different world now for aspiring potters.
Modern homes put little emphasis on handmade British
tableware or collectable ceramics. Mass production in
Asia fulfils the need for functional and decorative crockery.
Art is seen as something for the rich. It is harder than ever
to carve out a niche.

Back to the day job – sponging the large fish and sea surf bottle first seen on page 7

But pottery will prevail. It has for millennia. As long as there is clay, someone will want to mould it to their own design. Someone else will want to buy it. The wheel will continue to turn.

To succeed, potters need to think and do. They need to be artists and scientists. Roger Cockram meets all the criteria, and we look forward to accompanying him on the rest of his journey. ●

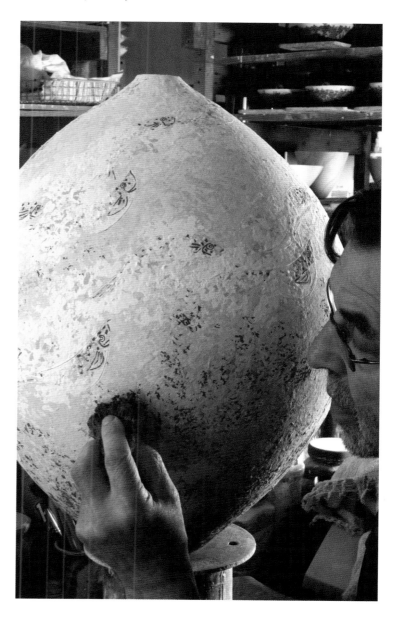

...also mentioned

Page numbers indicate first mention